MUSIC

KAY ROWLEY

ROCK WORLD

Crestwood House
New York

ROCK WORLD

ROCK CONCERTS
ROCK MUSIC
ROCK STARS
ROCK VIDEOS

EDITOR: James Kerr
SERIES DESIGNER: Helen White
COVER:DJ Jazzy Jeff and (right) the Fresh Prince. From being a rapper, the Fresh Prince has gone on to star in his own TV show.

First published in Great Britain in 1991 by
Wayland (Publishers) Ltd
61 Western Road, Hove
East Sussex BN3 1JD

First published in the United States in 1992 by
Crestwood House
Macmillan Publishing Company
866 Third Avenue
New York, NY 10022

Macmillan Publishing Company is part of the Maxwell
Macmillan Communication Group of Companies.

© Copyright 1991 Wayland (Publishers) Ltd

First Edition
Printed in Italy by G. Canale & C.S.p.A., Turin
10 9 8 7 6 5 4 3 2 1

Rowley, Kay.
    Rock music / by Kay Rowley.—1st ed.
        p.   cm.—(Rock world)
    Includes bibliographical references and index.
    Summary: A history of rock music, its origins, its stars, its different styles, and its impact on a generation.
        ISBN 0-89686-714-5
        1. Rock music—History and criticism—Juvenile literature.
    [1. Rock music—History and criticism.]   I. Title.   II. Series
    Rowley, Kay. Rock world.
    ML3534.R718   1992
    781-66'09—dc20

91-22085
CIP
AC MN

CONTENTS

INTRO

IF YOU TAKE a look at the top 20 singles in the music charts at any given time, you will see examples of many different styles of music. Very often the pioneers and originators of a particular musical style are unaware of setting a trend; that's usually for the historians and journalists to sort out afterward.

For the purposes of this book, we can say that a trend, or rock fad, is one that appeals to a certain section of the musically aware public. In fact, the description "rock fad" usually ends up as a contradiction in terms. Once a new movement in music has caught the attention of the record-buying public, it ceases to be a minority interest and inevitably bows to the pressures of commercialization. Apart from these pressures, one

Rock musician David Byrne of the Talking Heads.

common feature that unites all the major developments in popular music is a gradual change or growth, or evolution. No musical form has simply popped up out of the blue, even though it may sometimes seem that way.

The sort of things that can influence writers and performers are many and varied, but usually musical change comes about through some sort of revolt against the current fashion. Sometimes it is violent, as, for example, punk or bebop jazz. Other times it is just the reverse. By taking a look back over the 20th century, we can see how the various styles evolved.

The first major change to popular music came at around the time of World War I. This change came in the form of jazz, black music from the southern United States, centered around New Orleans. It was originally a mixture of African slave songs and rhythms. But the beginning of the 20th century saw it blending with existing European musical forms such as waltzes and marches. Jazz revolutionized dance music. All the dance crazes of the 1920s, such as the Charleston, were simply watered down forms of Dixieland (traditional) jazz.

In the 1930s, jazz was beginning to be recognized as a serious art form, helped by composers such as Duke Ellington. He wrote jazz scores for symphony orchestras as well as more popular pieces. By the beginning of the 1940s some of the young jazz musicians, such as Dizzy Gillespie and Charlie Parker, were exploring new forms, feeling that jazz had stagnated.

The result of their exploration was bebop. This burst upon the scene around 1945, causing a split between both musicians and fans.

The mod revival of the early 1980s gave a new lease of life to the mod accessory – the scooter.

The movement lasted a relatively short time, but it changed the face of jazz forever. Fans of the new jazz were called modernists or, as they later became known in the 1960s, mods.

Over the last 30 years jazz has managed to co-exist with rock, sometimes influencing it, sometimes being influenced by it. In the 1960s traditional jazz was briefly resurrected by the likes of Acker Bilk and Kenny Ball, and in the 1970s the jazz vocal group Manhattan Transfer scored several big rock chart hits. Jazz fusion (jazz/rock, jazz/funk, Latin/jazz) has also given birth to some crossover successes like Spyro Gyra and the Crusaders.

Jazz musicians usually have an easier time crossing over into rock (e.g., Herbie Hancock, George Benson, Quincy Jones, Bobby McFerrin) than the other way around. This is mostly because in jazz more emphasis is placed on musicianship than image. Those rock artists who have made brave attempts to enter the world of jazz (e.g., Sting, Joe Jackson, Joni Mitchell, Alison Moyet and Swing Out Sister) have found that their efforts have met with varying degrees of success.

What of the other influences on rock music over the last 80 years? The list is enormous, ranging from stage (and later film) musicals to traditional folk music, both white and black. In the rest of this book, some of the more influential movements will be examined.

ROCK AND ROLL is undoubtedly the first true musical fad. The name was originally coined by DJ Alan Freed for his 1952 radio show *Moondog's Rock 'n' Roll Party*. As well as the popular white hits of the day, Freed liked to include the latest black rhythm and blues (R&B) sounds and wanted a name for his show that would avoid any racial overtones. The show was an enormous success and Freed became a household name, later appearing in three movies – *Rock Around the Clock*; *Rock, Rock, Rock* and *Don't Knock the Rock*.

As a musical form, rock and roll is a combination of white rockabilly and black R&B, terms that probably need some explanation of their own. In the 1950s rockabilly represented the latest step in the evolution of white American country music. This had its roots in 19th-century European folk music. As musicians moved away from traditional tunes by composing their own, the music became totally Americanized.

In the 1930s, country music was heard for the first time outside its stronghold in the southern United States when singing cowboys, such as Gene Autry and Roy Rogers, appeared in movies and

subsequently became internationally known stars.

Each state had developed its own style. There was bluegrass from Kentucky, cajun from Louisiana, and there were variations like Western Swing, which included jazz, blues and ballads. By the early 1950s, the old-style hillbilly instruments such as the accordion, fiddle and banjo had given way to a new lineup of guitar, upright bass, piano and drums. The music, although still recognizably country, was more upbeat and showed the growing influence of black blues styles such as R&B.

R&B was the later, more sophisticated version of the original Delta blues played in Mississippi around the 1920s and

ABOVE: The Stray Cats revived rockabilly in the early 1980s.

1930s. After World War II, many black people migrated from the South to places such as Chicago, taking with them their rural, acoustic blues. Once in the city, however, the music changed to suit the surroundings, becoming amplified and more uptempo.

In 1951, "Rocket 88," generally acknowledged to be the first rock and roll record, was released. Recorded by Jackie Brenston and the Kings of Rhythm for Chicago's famous Chess label, the single marked the debut of band member Ike Turner (later husband of Tina).

Ike (playing guitar) and Tina Turner. Although Ike was one of the first rock and rollers, this photograph was taken when the couple's music and clothing were more typical of black soul artists'.

Aspiring singers such as Elvis Presley and Jerry Lee Lewis were excited by this new music that they heard in clubs and on the radio, and they started incorporating its phrasing into their own style. When Presley was recording his first single in 1954, instead of singing a new country song that studio owner Sam Phillips had acquired, Elvis launched into a black R&B song, "That's Alright Mama." Phillips immediately recognized what a phenomenon Presley was: a white boy who could sing powerfully enough not to dilute the raw power of the original version.

Beating Presley to it as the first white rock and roller was Bill Haley. He had already covered "Rocket 88" in an aggressive rockabilly style back in 1951 and had a small hit with another R&B copy, "Rock the Joint," in 1952. Sensing that rockabilly was the coming thing, he dropped his hillbilly image and changed his band's name from the Saddlemen to the Comets to record "Crazy Man Crazy" in 1953. In 1954 he had another hit with "Rock Around the Clock," following it up with "Shake Rattle & Roll," which became a top ten hit in both the United States and Britain.

After this, Haley temporarily disappeared from the British charts, making it seem as though rock and roll had just been a passing craze. However, when "Rock Around the Clock" was included in the movie *Blackboard Jungle* in 1955, the record was re-released and rocketed to number one. During 1956 Haley enjoyed eight more hit records plus an album, *Bill Haley's Rock and Roll Show*, which also made it into the singles chart.

When Haley finally arrived in Britain to tour in 1957, however, it proved to be his undoing. The teenagers who had bought his records saw that he was, in reality, a chubby, married, 30-year-old: hardly the ingredients needed to be a teen idol.

The man who took his place was Elvis Presley. By the end of 1956, Elvis had chalked up five British hits and had appeared in his first movie, *Love Me Tender*. At the end of the movie his character dies:

Bill Haley and the Comets. Bill Haley is wearing a green jacket, although you can also spot him by his trademark kiss curl.

James Dean has remained a cult figure right up to the present day.

as much – if not more – success, but as a pop singer rather than a rocker.

The heyday of rock and roll lasted only three short years, but it produced some inspired entertainers including Little Richard, Jerry Lee Lewis, Buddy Holly, the Everly Brothers, Gene Vincent, Eddie Cochran and Chuck Berry. It was the very first rock music sung by the young for the young, and as such had an influence that reached way beyond the average music craze.

By the mid-1950s, the economies of Britain and Europe were at last recovering from World War II, and for the first time in years people had money to spend on luxuries such as records and fashions. New, young movie stars such as James Dean and Marlon Brando exploded on the scene in fast cars and motorcycle leather, a far cry from the tweeds and oxfords of their parents.

In Britain in the 1950s, rock and roll inspired the teddy boy look, a throwback to the Edwardian fashions of velvet-collared jackets, silk-patterned waistcoats and long hairstyles with exaggerated sideburns. Completing the teddy boy outfit were tight black slacks (drainpipes) and massive crepe-

Hundreds of teenage girls up and down Britain were treated by the St. John's Ambulance Brigade for fainting and shock.

Britain never really produced anyone to rival Presley. Tommy Steele looked too happy to be taken seriously as a rocker and Cliff Richard didn't appear on the scene until 1958. By this time Elvis had been drafted into the army, and rock and roll was on its last legs. When Presley returned in 1960, he resumed his recording career with

soled suede shoes or very pointed black leather boots (winklepickers).

In the 1960s, motorcycle greasers, or "rockers," took over from "teds" in supporting what they saw to be real rock and roll. They frequently came to blows in style wars with mods on scooters whose tastes included anything from modern jazz through rock steady (an early form of reggae) to R&B. The progressive music of the late 1960s almost sounded the death knell of rock and roll, but in the mid-1970s it got a new champion in the person of Bruce Springsteen.

Rockabilly, too, was momentarily revived in the 1980s by the Stray Cats and one or two other groups. Elvis copyist Shakin' Stevens also had a good run of top 20 hits. With the launch of the new oldies radio stations toward the end of the decade, rock and roll once more got a reprieve.

Lots of performers – be they Cliff Richard, Jon Bon Jovi or Billy Idol – still add one or two old rockers to their live performance encores, knowing these will always get an audience to its feet.

As recently as 1990, Elvis's 1957 hit "All Shook Up" got an electronic kiss of life from Adamski, although it must be admitted that it sounded nothing like the original.

The ted uniform: crepe-soled shoes, velvet-collared jacket, shoelace tie and forehead curl.

SOUL

SOUL MUSIC grew out of a mixture of jazz, blues and gospel at more or less the same time rock and roll came on the scene. To many black people, the old-style blues reminded them too much of their enslaved and downtrodden past, so they welcomed this new dance music as a sign of an upturn in their fortunes. Unfortunately soul music is often pretty unsoulful, with singers just going through the motions. However, in the hands of experts such as Otis Redding, Aretha Franklin or James Brown ("the Godfather of Soul"), it can be so moving as to be spine-chilling.

James Brown was born into a poor family in Macon, Georgia, in 1933 and as a child sang in church. In 1954 he formed a vocal group, the Famous Flames, which performed gospel songs. During the next few years he had a couple of minor hits. The turning point came in 1958 with the gospel-flavored "Try Me," which became a national hit. He disbanded the group, put together a new band and used his gospel phrasing and emotional delivery to add zest to what were often average R&B numbers.

By the early 1960s James had expanded the Famous Flames into an entire revue with dancers, singers, a large band and support acts. As well as being a mesmerizing singer, Brown was a brilliant dancer and first-rate showman. As a ten-year-old child, Prince was taken to see Brown, and he later used Brown's routines as the basis of his own stage show.

In 1962 Brown's *Live at the Apollo* LP became a million seller, an unprecedented achievement for an R&B record. Throughout the 1960s he remained the number one black superstar. With his 1968 hit,

James Brown's cult status increased in the 1980s when rap artists used his music to rap to.

"Say It Loud – I'm Black & I'm Proud," he became a figurehead for the black consciousness movement.

During the 1970s his influence extended to bands such as Sly & the Family Stone, Kool & the Gang, Earth Wind & Fire and Parliament/Funkadelic. These bands drew on Brown's repertoire to create a new type of funky dance music. In 1981, Brown himself bounced back (at the age of 48) with "Rap Payback," his answer to the New York rapper movement. In 1986 he scored his biggest British hit with "Living in America." In the United States his tally of almost 50 top 40 hits is surpassed only by Elvis and the Beatles.

Looking for vintage soul music on LPs is a hit-or-miss affair. Motown is often mistakenly described as a soul label, and though it has had some soulful artists like Gladys Knight and Marvin Gaye, most of the music is unashamedly black rock aimed at crossover audiences. One of the best record labels on which to find good soul music is Atlantic, which is now part of the Warner Bros. empire.

Deee-lite has revived the fashions associated with 1970s soul music.

13

Following its original R&B releases in the late 1940s, Atlantic took on gospel-flavored singers such as Ruth Brown, LaVern Baker and Ray Charles, plus popular black vocal groups such as the Coasters and the Drifters. As well as its own artists, it distributed Stax/Volt (a Memphis soul/R&B label) featuring, among others, Otis Redding, Sam & Dave and Percy Sledge.

In 1967 Atlantic signed up a 25-year-old singer named Aretha Franklin who had been recording without success since her teens. Her first Atlantic release, "I Never Loved a Man," was a masterpiece, and over the next year she had six more hit singles, including "Respect" and "Chain of Fools." During the 1970s her output became erratic, and after 1974 there was an 11-year gap before the "Queen of Soul" once again occupied the charts.

The 1970s were uncertain times for soul music. Along the way it had been hijacked by a lot of syrupy vocal groups and singers such as the Detroit Spinners, Harold Melvin & the Bluenotes and Barry White – all displaying technique and no feeling. When disco came along, soul temporarily went into eclipse.

By the 1980s, a whole new generation of singers was acknowledging its debt to 1960s soul music. It included the Style Council, Paul Young, George Michael, Annie Lennox, Phil Collins and Hall & Oates. In 1984 a soul sister of Aretha's, Tina Turner, embarked on a new career at the age of 46 when her *Private Dancer* LP became one of the best-sellers of the year.

As we move into the 1990s, soul music is once again in vogue with groups such as Soul II Soul and the Chimes, and solo artists such as Anita Baker, Mica Paris and Lisa Stansfield.

Soul II Soul started out as a cult band, playing to small audiences at the Fridge, a club in London. They are now internationally known.

HIP HOP&HOUSE

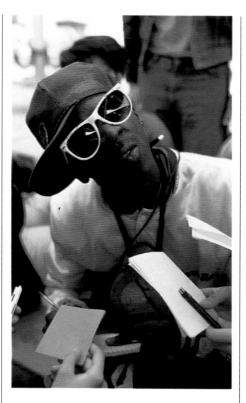

BY THE END of the 1970s the disco boom had peaked. The original slower dance rhythm of "The Hustle" (Van McCoy, 1975) had been superceded by high-energy hits such as Sylvester's "Mighty Real" (revived in 1990 by Jimmy Somerville). Everyone, including unlikely artists such as Barbra Streisand, had made disco records. The result was overkill.

As a direct reaction, hip hop was about as far away from the whole disco scene as it was possible to get. Where disco's audience had been predominantly white, aged 24 to 35, hip hop was exclusively black and aimed at people in their late teens to early twenties. In many cases disco was close enough to rock music to receive a lot of radio airplay. Hip hop, however, was based on rhythm and rap and at the beginning could be heard only in clubs.

The rapper scene originated in New York where club DJs had developed and extended the stylized, rhythmic form of speech they used to introduce records. This was the American version of Jamaican "toasting" (see later Reggae section). This in turn is an adaptation of a much older African tribal tradition of recounting stories. The earliest examples of rap on record are by the Last Poets and Gil Scott-Heron, and date back to the early 1970s.

The original accompaniment to the rap was just a fairly slow drum rhythm. This was later augmented by a looped lick, i.e., a musical phrase borrowed, or "sampled," from an existing record, which would be taped and repeated at regular intervals.

At first a lot of the early hip hop records by bands such as Grandmaster Flash, Melle Mel & the Furious Five and the Sugarhill

Gang featured music played on real instruments. However, this was an expensive way to record. Many young aspiring hip hop artists who were not musicians realized they could perform most of the music themselves. All they needed were simple and relatively cheap electronic equipment, such as drum machines and sequencers.

There were also various tricks such as "scratching" and "transforming" to be learned from the DJs. Scratching is the manipulation by hand of records on the turntable. Using two copies of the same record on a double turntable, the DJ could, for instance, extend an eight-bar introduction to sixteen bars, then jump straight to the end of the record. Also, by pulling and pushing the record, the voice or instrument pitch and sound could be drastically altered or slowed down. To hear what can be done, listen to Chaka Khan's "I Feel for You" and Salt 'n' Pepa's "Push It."

Transforming is the mechanical equivalent of moving the fader switches up and down in order to get a sort of Morse code effect over the record; this works particularly well with string sections.

House music first appeared in the mid-1980s and, like hip hop, was DJ- rather than musician-led. Its inspirational home was Chicago, where young DJs who wanted to create their own disco music started making records. Using the Japanese Roland 909 drum machine to produce an obviously synthetic drum sound of around 120 to 123 beats to the bar, the DJs added layers of rhythmic rather than melodic sequences using other low-cost synthesizers.

Very soon there were several variations, for example, hip house, which is rap over a house beat, and

ABOVE: Cash Money and DJ Marvelous demonstrate what you need to scratch – two turntables, two copies of the same record and quick fingers.

OPPOSITE: Flavor Flav of Public Enemy – a band that has enjoyed mainstream success without toning down its hardcore sound.

acid house. This is named after the so-called psychedelic music of the late 1960s (see next section on progressive music). These types of music made use of electronic effects, added at the mixing stage of a record to produce strange noises or note distortions. For acid house, the process was rather more low budget. It used a Roland 303, which is a little box, not much bigger than six inches square, costing around $150. It consists of a single oscillator that, when the pitch is altered, generates strange sounds.

The return of the "peace and love" ethic of the 1960s has also influenced the rappers. Many of them have moved away from their original, aggressive urban obsessions to more environmental and social issues. As hip hop and house styles have been absorbed into the mainstream of rock, commercialized versions turn up in the charts by both white and black artists. Some remain close to their club origins. Others, such as Partners in Kryme's "Turtle Power," M. C. Hammer's "You Can't Touch This" and Deee-lite's "Groove Is in the Heart," are true rock crossovers – a sure sign that these are no longer fad records.

NO MUSICAL STYLE bursts upon the scene without warning. There is always a formative period where all the elements start to come together. Progressive music, sometimes called acid rock or psychedelic music, did not simply appear overnight fully formed. It was two or three years in the making. Two of the major factors in its development were the programming changes on American radio and the so-called "British invasion" of the United States in the mid-1960s.

In 1966 a ratings war among commercial stations had resulted in a drastic reduction of the number of records being aired. This made it hard for new bands to get any exposure. At the same time, there were more bands than ever before, a grassroots response to the waves of British bands that toured the United States in the wake of the Beatles and the Rolling Stones.

These groups, often called punk, or garage, bands, performed a fairly unsophisticated form of rock characterized by fuzztone on the guitar sound and anti-social lyrics. Their records were mostly recorded for small, local labels; few received any radio-play. These were the pioneers of progressive, or "underground," music.

In 1967 when FM radio was launched, those bands whose interest lay beyond making rock singles suddenly had a chance to be heard. In an attempt to get as far away as possible from top 40 hits, DJs played a mix of classical, Eastern music, jazz, electronic music, folk, country and R&B. The bands themselves started experimenting with unusual instruments, such as the Indian sitar, and with different musical styles. Some bands, for instance, the Doors and the Velvet Underground, even incorporated poetry and recitation.

ABOVE:
Progressive/
punk artist
Iggy Pop.

As with any musical trend, the best and most original performers represent only a small percentage of the whole. These are usually the survivors. Bands that are still around today or whose reputations live on include the Doors, the

Grateful Dead, the Steve Miller Band, ZZ Top and Jefferson Starship. Many of the more "progressive" bands were just too pretentious, had silly names such as Moby Grape, and insisted on playing long, rambling pieces like classical "suites," which bored everyone to death.

Within progressive music, the main influences had been country rock, blues and hard rock, later to be renamed heavy metal. By the early 1970s these various styles were attracting completely different audiences, and the general trend was once again moving toward commercial rock. Only heavy metal held out against it.

HEAVY METAL

IN MANY WAYS, the term "heavy metal" is as all-embracing as the label "progressive," including as it does everything from glam rock to southern boogie. In the 1980s it fragmented still further, and purists claim that real heavy metal no longer exists. However, for the sake of convenience, that's what we'll call it here.

The origins of heavy metal can be traced back to virtually one 1960s British R&B band, the Yardbirds. This band produced three guitar heroes in rapid succession – Eric Clapton, Jeff Beck and Jimmy Page. These three, along with Jimi Hendrix, became the inspiration for all of the British and American hard rock guitar-led bands that followed.

Clapton's next group, Cream, started the fashion for long, loud guitar solos set against relentless bass accompaniment and thunderous drumming – a style that has been much imitated but never equaled. When Cream split up in 1968, its place was filled by Jimmy Page's Led Zeppelin, which played even longer and louder. Zeppelin's reign lasted for 12 years, until 1980, during which time various strains of heavy metal came and went. Much 1970s American heavy

metal was pomp rock, i.e., loud, stadium rock and roll as produced by the likes of Boston or REO Speedwagon. Other bands that have been placed in this category, Lynyrd Skynyrd, for example, played overloud southern boogie. In Britain pomp rock's closest relative was pop metal, typified by Ritchie Blackmore's Rainbow and Queen.

In Britain in the early 1970s, glam rock swept the country with Gary Glitter and bands such as

ABOVE: *Jimi Hendrix's early death contributed to his cult status.*

21

Slade and Sweet. This movement, however, never caught on in the United States. Only in the early 1980s did the newer wave of American heavy metalers such as Mötley Crüe and Poison, who wore exaggerated makeup and outrageous costumes, acknowledge glam rock's influence.

Mötley Crüe is a band whose image owes a lot to the glam rock era.

In the late 1970s the British punk movement, which like heavy metal helped kids vent their aggression and frustration through loud music, inspired a few bands like Iron Maiden and Saxon. Generally, though, it drove heavy metal back underground from where it came. When it resurfaced in the early 1980s new bands such as Def Leppard and Hanoi Rocks brought fresh energy to the genre, and its popularity – which had remained strong in Britain, the United States and Japan – spread to the rest of the world.

By the mid-1980s, metal fragmented still further with the emergence of thrash metal, a brash style, played fast and furiously by bands such as Metallica and Megadeth. This has been offset by the increasing number of socially and environmentally conscious bands such as Skid Row and Warrant. These groups have used their popularity to speak out against street violence and the destruction of the planet.

Heavy metal bands have always had a reputation among non-devotees as boneheads playing for fans of very little brain. This is, on the whole, quite unjustified. Many of the musicians, for example, Robert Plant, Jani Lane and Bruce Dickenson, are intelligent and articulate. In some cases, such as guitarist Eddie Van Halen, they are even conservatory trained.

Another undeserved stigma is the media's claim that heavy metal bands advocate devil worship. While it is true that they often have

savage names – Slayer, Scorpions, Poison – and their album covers frequently depict grisly scenes of death and destruction, this is merely part of a fantastic, almost comic book image, enjoyed by their fans.

Traditionally, heavy metal has been the preserve of white male performers. In recent years, however, quite a few female groups have emerged, such as Femme Fatale and Vixen, as well as the first black group, Living Colour.

For the most part heavy metal bands and artists prefer to avoid the commercial world of rock, but when they do cross over, like Guns 'n' Roses or Jon Bon Jovi, they show themselves competent to sing as well as scream.

LEFT: Anthrax.

BELOW: The black rock group Living Colour.

PUNK

CONFUSINGLY ENOUGH there have been three punk movements, two in the United States and one in Britain toward the end of the 1970s. The first movement is covered in the chapter on progressive music. Except for a few bands, such as the Kingsmen ("Louie Louie"), and ? and the Mysterians (their "96 Tears" was covered in 1990 by a later punk band the Stranglers), the music was pretty awful.

Punks are perhaps the most recognizable cult fans.

The second punk movement came in the mid-1970s in the United States, specifically from New York, where bands such as Television, Blondie, Patti Smith, Talking Heads and the Ramones were regulars of the new wave club CBGBs. In 1976 the Ramones visited Britain, heavily influencing the flood of new wave bands with their high speed, minimalist rock (anything up to 17 songs in half an hour) and their scruffy uniform of beat-up black leather jackets and torn jeans.

Despite the punk label, American new wave was generally more melodic than its British counterpart. The perfect example was Blondie's Debbie Harry, who became a major rock star by the end of the 1970s. Talking Heads, too, quickly shook off their original punk tag and made a series of best-selling, quirky-but-fun albums and videos throughout the 1980s.

Probably the most notorious group to come out of the British new wave movement of 1976-78 was the Sex Pistols. Masterminded by Malcolm McLaren, who had already managed American glam rockers the New York Dolls, the Pistols were the epitome of the new order. Their ripped clothing held together with safety pins, their basic sound system and their anarchic stance were a violent reaction

Finally they found a home with Virgin Records and had 11 hit singles over the next three years. In 1978, Lydon departed and formed a new group called Public Image Ltd (PIL), which chalked up three top 20 hits.

LEFT: The key members of the Sex Pistols: Sid Vicious (left) and Johnny Rotten.

BELOW: Siouxsie's "gothic" look.

against the established supergroups and the music business.

Onstage, singer Johnny Rotten (John Lydon) would incite the audience to riot. As a result the group was banned from several London clubs. In November 1977 they were signed to EMI Records for $60,000. However, within a short time they had made the headlines by swearing on a live TV show, and they were fired by the label. They were immediately picked up by A&M Records for $100,000, only to be dropped in a matter of days – surely the shortest recording contract ever.

Damned, the Clash, the Jam and the Stranglers, were, with the exception of the Clash, never truly punk in the first place. The Stranglers were pop-like, the Damned were a mannered glam rock band and the Jam an R&B/soul-inspired group whose leader, Paul Weller, subsequently founded the Style Council.

Punk was the first rock movement in which there was real equality of the sexes. Plenty of women like Siouxsie (& the Banshees), Nina Hagen, Joan Jett (the Runaways) and Tina Weymouth (Talking Heads) grabbed the opportunity to play rock and roll rather than listen to it.

Punk was not a movement that produced many superstars: Probably the closest is Billy Idol from Generation X. Musically it did not have much lasting impact either. What it *did* do was shake the entire music business out of its complacency, giving birth to a lot of small independent record labels. These were run by people who were more in touch with what the fans really wanted. They also gave a lot of musicians – who would otherwise never have stood a chance – the opportunity to record.

The very amateurism of the Pistols proved to be an inspiration for would-be musicians from east to west wanting to get on stage too. "I don't know how, I just did" said Poly Styrene of X-Ray Spex. "It was just at that time when anyone could form a band." Of the literally hundreds of bands that popped up, few survived the decline of punk in 1978. Those that did, such as the

REGGAE

IN THE 1990s reggae has been increasingly accepted within rock culture. Reggae stars Aswad and Maxi Priest regularly turn up in the rock charts, and reggae itself is no longer exclusively black – as was seen from the Beats International number one "Dub Be Good to Me."

However, this has not always been the case; reggae started off as very much a musical style written by Jamaicans for Jamaicans. Although it was mostly Afro-Caribbean in origin, a rhythmic progression from the musical style calypso, it also owed something to zydeco – French-influenced black R&B from Louisiana.

In 1960, the Bluebeat label was set up in Britain to provide West Indian immigrants with home-grown music. Among the various styles was an offbeat, loping dance music called ska. This gradually became popular with white teenagers, especially mods. In 1964 this music fashion, now called bluebeat, reached the white rock charts with Millie Small's "My Boy Lollipop" and Ezz Reco and the Launchers' "King of Kings."

Ska, meanwhile, was transforming itself into rock steady, a more uptempo and polished version of its predecessor. In 1967 Desmond Dekker had the first rock steady hit with "007 (Shanty Town)," followed by several big hits in 1969 and 1970. Among these was a number one, "Israelites," which re-emerged in the late 1980s (with different words) as TV advertisements for two separate products. Another Jamaican artist to make an impression on the rock charts around this time was Jimmy Cliff.

At the same time as commercial rock steady was reaching an international audience, many Jamaicans were going back to their African roots to look for self-expression. Some had espoused the Rastafarian religion, wore

Beats International.

27

dreadlocks (long, braided hair) and sang of Zion, their ancestral home of Ethiopia. This was the beginning of reggae.

In both Jamaica and Britain, club DJs with their massive sound systems had always been very influential and had developed a style of talking over the records they played. These "raps," or toasting, as it is called, could be just self-advertising or about more consciousness-raising subjects such as black rights or brotherly love. Special "dub" backing tracks were recorded, often with lots of feedback, consisting of bass and drums with occasional instrumental

bursts. Although enormously popular in Jamaica, this style of reggae remained a cult interest in other places.

By the beginning of the 1970s, the rock charts contained quite a few commercial reggae records including one by an American singer Johnny Nash called "I Can See Clearly Now" (covered in 1990 by Hothouse Flowers). Backing Nash was a band called Sons of the Jungle, which subsequently became known as Bob Marley & the Wailers.

Marley was reggae's only real international superstar, and until his early death at the age of 35 in 1981, he made reggae accessible to white audiences worldwide while never losing touch with his Jamaican roots. One of his songs, "I Shot the Sheriff," was a top ten hit for Eric Clapton in 1974 and again in 1982.

Toward the end of the 1970s, old-style ska, or rock steady, was revived by several bands that boasted a multiracial lineup. Chief among them were the Specials, Bad Manners, the Beat and UB40. The most commercially successful band playing this type of music was Madness, a north London group that named itself after a big

Young Jamaicans at a reggae concert. The man on the right wears a hat with green, gold and red trim – the colors associated with the Rastafarian religion and Zion.

George & Culture Club and Grace Jones. As a reaction against its commercialization, a number of British-born black musicians have tried to maintain the music's original spirit. Because of this, reggae has once more reverted to its cult status.

hit by Prince Buster, one of ska's original leading lights.

Much of the initial message of these bands was concerned with social issues such as unemployment among the young or with racial tension. By the early part of the 1980s, however, the bands that still remained had become less radical. In 1983 two members of the Beat went off to form Fine Young Cannibals, and of the rest of the bands only UB40 still exists.

By now the influence of reggae had permeated the whole of the rock scene, and its distinctive offbeat rhythms could be heard in rock songs by Blondie, Boy

GLOSSARY

Acoustic instrument Instrument played without amplification.

Anarchic Insubordinate or rebellious.

Anti-social Rebellious or anti-establishment.

Bebop A form of modern jazz started during the 1940s by Charlie Parker and Dizzy Gillespie.

Blues Originally Afro-American songs dating from the turn of the century; often accompanied by an acoustic guitar.

Calypso Songs of Afro-Caribbean origin. They often concern topical events and the singers frequently make up the lyrics as they go along.

Charleston A 1920s dance craze.

Commercialization Turning a project into a moneymaking concern.

Dixieland jazz Often called traditional jazz. It originated around New Orleans just before World War I.

Edwardian Relating to the reign of Edward VII (1901-10).

Fader An electronic recording control that fades the sound in and out.

Fuzztone A rough, distorted sound.

Gospel Religious music originally performed by black Americans.

Minimalist rock With only the basic tunes and rhythms.

Mods Abbreviation for "modernists." They were originally devotees of modern jazz, but later represented a teenage fashion movement of the early 1960s.

Oscillator A transmitter that puts out vibrating sounds.

Phrasing The rendering of musical notes in a certain manner, e.g., blues phrasing, jazz phrasing, etc.

Rastafarian A Jamaican movement claiming Ethiopian Emperor Haile Selassie (Ras Tafari) as "the living God."

Ratings A way of measuring popularity among listeners.

Sequencer An electronic keyboard synthesizing the sounds of various instruments. It can play a sequence of notes at the touch of one key.

Sitar A large, stringed instrument from India.

Stylized Played in a particular style or exaggerated way.

Synthetic sound Sounding the same as the original, but not using original instruments.

READING LIST

Blocher, Arlo. *Rock*. New Jersey: Troll, 1976.

Busnar, Gene. *It's Rock 'n' Roll*. New York: Messner, 1979.

Bygrave, Mike. *Rock*. London: Hamilton, 1977.

David, Andrew. *Rock Stars: People at the Top of the Charts*. New York: Exeter Books. 1979.

Fornatale, Peter. *The Story of Rock 'n' Roll*. New York: William Morrow, 1987.

Lane, Peter. *What Rock Is All About*. New York: Messner, 1979.

Meigs, James B. and Jennifer Stern. *Make Your Own Music Video*. New York: Franklin Watts, 1986.

MTV Presents 2nd Annual MTV Video Music Awards. New Jersey: Warner Bros. Publications, 1985.

Nite, Norm N. *Rock On: The Illustrated Encyclopedia of Rock 'n' Roll: The Video Revolution, 1978-Present*. New York: Harper & Row, 1985.

Paige, David. *A Day in the Life of a Rock Musician*. New Jersey: Troll, 1980.

Van der Horst, Brian. *Rock Music*. New York: Franklin Watts, 1973.

White, Timothy. *Rock Stars*. New York: Stewart, Tabori & Chang, 1984.

PICTURE ACKNOWLEDGMENTS

All Action 18 (right), 24; London Features International (Ron Wolfson) COVER, 6, 8, 10, (Phil Loftus) 15, (Andy Catlin) 17, 18 (left), (Derek Ridgers) 25 (right), (Tom Sheehan) 27, 28; MCA (Henry Dilitz) 20 (top); Redferns (David Redfern) 9, 12, 29 (left); Rex Features (Ilpo Musto) 4, (Paul Brown) 5, (Richard Pasley) 7, 11, 13, 14, 16, 19, (Joel Elkins) 21, (Fabio Nosotti) 22, 23, 26, (Dave Hogan) 29 (right).

INDEX